Just Because

Growing Old,

It Doesn't Mean

That You Have To

Grow Up

A book of whimsical poetry

by

A.B.Wyze

2021

ISBN
9798739734792

Book
One

CONTENTS

DAYS WHEN

I went to my Mother I said, "I've a question."
She said, "Ok sonny, just ask it."
I said, "When I go to the hen house each day
  should I put all the eggs in one basket?"

There are days when you do
there are days when you don't.
There are days when you haven't a clue.
But try to remember
on days that you don't
that you don't have a day when you DO!

My sister got married, the eighth time to date,
but we knew it would end up in doom.
The wedding went well, the reception was short,
she ran off with a friend of the groom.

There are days that you will
there are days that you won't.
There are days that you should stay in bed.
But try to remember
on days that you won't
that you've not made a vow to get wed.

My neighbour said smoking is good for your health,
and to say that it's not is a joke.
He lit a cigar, whilst fuelling his car,
with a bang, he just went up in smoke.

There are days that you're right,
there are days you are wrong.
There are days when your memory sticks.
But try to remember
on days you are wrong
that petrol and lighters don't mix.

My mum gave me such a hard whack of the ear
that it turned such a bright shade of red.
"You are just like your father," she said with a frown,
"just a little bit soft in the head."

There are days when you do,
there are days when you don't.
There are days when you haven't a clue.
But try to remember on days that you don't
that you don't have a day when you do.

BELIEVING

Believing in tigers is easy,
as they can be seen at the zoo.
Believing in leopards is simple,
for they can be spotted there too.
Believing in moles is much harder,
they live underground, out of sight.
Believing in bats is quite tricky,
as they only come out at night.
Believing in things that you can't see,
takes lots of faith, so my mum said.
So I won't be turning my light out,
until I've checked under my bed.

THE LONELY GIANT

Oh, the giant was lonely, he sat in his cave
and he stared at the grey rocky walls.
"I have lived here for ages," he said with a moan,
"I've a doorway but nobody calls."

So, the giant walked out to the edge of the ledge
and he gave out a mournful old groan.
"Oh it does not seem fair that I have such a view,
and I have to enjoy it alone."

And just then an idea it sparked in his brain
all at once he knew just what to do.
So, he put up a sign saying:
HOLIDAY LET
(Self-Contained with a marvellous view!)

Then he went back inside and he tidied his cave
and he swept up the discarded bones.
And he whistled and sang as he polished away
knowing soon he would not be alone.

And the giant was right just one hour went past
when he heard someone knock at his door.
When he opened it up, he got such a surprise...
no, he could not believe what he saw.

Such a wizened old crone with a tall pointed hat
and a broom which she used for support.
And he looked the crone up and he looked the crone down
"It's a witch," was the first thing he thought.

And the crone had a nose that was hooked like a beak
and she opened her mouth and she spoke.
"I would love to stay here if I may," she remarked,
with a squeak and a wheeze and a croak.

And her eyes were as pale as the palest of moons,
then they changed to a deep shade of blue.
And she turned to the ledge and she held up her broom,
and she said, "What a marvellous view."

"If you pay in advance," said the giant at once,
"you can stay for one day as a test.
For I know you're a witch and I'm not sure that I
would be safe with a witch for a guest."

So she paid him in gold from a pouch in her cloak,
and she paid not for one day but two.
Then she went to her room with its window so wide
and she stared at the marvellous view.

Then a knock on the door made the giant look up
and he opened that door really wide.
And he froze from his hair to the nails on his toes
for a dragon was standing outside.

"Pardon me," said the beast as it burped out a flame,
"but your sign caught my eye as I flew.
I would love to stay here for in all my born days
I've not seen such a marvellous view."

"If you pay in advance," said the giant at once,
"you can stay for one day as a test.
After all you're a dragon and I am in doubt,
it is safe to have you as a guest."

So the dragon agreed to the giant's request
and it paid with a sovereign or two.
And it went to its room with its window so wide
and it stared at the marvellous view.

When the evening came round they all sat on the ledge
by a fire that the dragon had made.
And they each told a tale of adventures they'd had
and the giant felt no more afraid.

Both the dragon and witch did not stay for one day,
no, they stayed for a year, maybe two.
And each evening they sat on that ledge telling tales
as they shared in the marvellous view.

ANNE BOLEYN

You have to feel for Anne Boleyn
poor lady lost her head.
Seems to me her only crime
was getting blooming wed.
And then of course the big mistake
that sent her husband wild.
She had the audacity
to bear a female child.
And that it seems was all it took
for Henry to see red.
And so they parted company...
as Anne did with her head.

THE ELEPHANT AND THE LEOPARD

The preacher was preaching, it's what preachers do,
his job title gives it away.
The elephant listened, it's what ears are for,
that preacher had so much to say.

He talked about animals, talked about man
he talked about Adam and Eve.
The elephant listened and then walked away
not sure of what he should believe.

The leopard, he lay in the shade of the tree,
the elephant sauntered his way.
"I know why you're spotty," he said to the cat.
"It's God who has made you this way."

The leopard peered out from the dark dappled shade
a curious look in his eye,
"God made the sunshine," he said with a snarl,
"what I'd like to ask Him is... why?"

The elephant sat on his haunches and smiled,
"We have to have sunshine," he said.
"For without the sunshine, we wouldn't have shade
and you would not have this cool bed."

"Everything's here for a reason," he said,
"and it's all down to God, I suppose."
"Then you'd better ask Him," the leopard remarked,
"why He gave you such a long nose."

A chimpanzee dropped from the branches above
and gave both the creatures a grin.
"I have an opinion," it said to them both,
"I'd love you to let me join in."

The tired old elephant looked at the chimp,
he wasn't a chimpanzee fan.
"You chimpanzees think you are better than us
because you can walk like a man!"

"You've got it my friend," said the young chimpanzee,
"It's called evolution you see.
And after an age of an age has passed by,
all men will be chimps just like me!"

The elephant sighed and he then gave a yawn,
he stared at the chimp in the tree.
"And all the small mice will grow trunks I suppose
and swell till they look just like me."

"What rubbish this is?" said the big spotted cat
who still hid away from the sun.
"If God wanted mice to have trunks my young friend
then He would have given them one."

"Oh my," said the chimp as he dropped to the ground,
"just listen to me I insist.
I'm asking you both to consider the fact
that God does not really exist."

"Oh my," said the leopard, "you're going too far
this hot sun has frazzled your brain."
"And I would agree," the old elephant sighed,
"you're going quite mad it is plain."

"It is just an idea," the chimpanzee said
as he climbed back up into the tree.
"And I cannot prove it for it will be years
before men look exactly like me."

The leopard he yawned as the chimp disappeared
and the elephant stood in the heat.
Just then a small mouse ran across the hot ground
and then stood in the shade at his feet.

"Excuse me," it squeaked at the top of its voice,
"you have not thought of this I suppose.
But I would look almost exactly like you
if I had a long trunk for a nose."

The elephant did not respond to the mouse
he went off for a walk in the sun.
The preacher had gone when he got back to town
and the children were out having fun.

He watched as a child ran across the hot sand,
saw it grab at the trunk of a tree.
It soon disappeared in the branches above
just as fast as a young chimpanzee.

THOSE WEASELS

Those weasels aren't so bad you know,
those weasels are alright.
They don't go drinking after hours
or get into a fight.
They don't sneak to the betting shop
and lose their weekly wage
or leer at lady weasels
who are roughly half their age.
A weasel picks a partner
and he stays with her for life.
Remember this the next you're called
a weasel by your wife!

DEAR MONDAY

Dear Monday
I'm glad that you're doing ok
you've been on my mind as of late.
You've never met Sunday,
despite being close,
but Monday, old Sunday's just great.
And if it's ok with you Monday old chum,
I'm not one for cramping your style
but Sunday and me
we have got things to do
he'd like to stay here for a while.
Now don't go and fly off the handle
old friend,
it's not such a problem at all.
I've spoken to Tuesday
and Tuesday said "Fine,"
he'll wait till we give him a call.
And you'll get a well-deserved break
my old mate,
a rest from the rush and the grind.
And hey, if you like it we'll do it some more,
I'm certain that Sunday won't mind.
Well thanks, that's just great,
you're an absolute star
I owe you one now me old chum.
So all it takes now is for somebody here
to get this explained to me Mum.

MRS BITM'KIT

You know Mrs Bitm'kit
she lives at twenty-six.
Wears her rollers to the shops
and walks with walking sticks.

You know Mrs Bitm'kit
she doesn't talk she shouts.
Drinks Rioja by the pint
and suffers from the gout.

You must know old Bitm'kit,
I can't recall her name.
Always has her slippers on
in sunshine or in rain.

Always shops on pension day
she's in the aisles by eight.
Searching for the knock down food
that's near its sell by date.

You know who I'm on about
her husband brought the pools.
Smelt like haddock three days old
and sharpened gardening tools.

Ah poor blighter passed away
they buried him in May.
Daren't have him cremated,
all that rum he put away.

You know Mrs Bitm'kit
she's well known round this place.
Pays for half a bingo card
and shares with Whatshisface.

Whatshisface? Yeah you know him
he does that paper round.
He's the bloke on Saturdays
sells programmes at the ground.

You wouldn't think to look at him
you wouldn't have a clue
but gossip is that Whatsisface
is worth a bob or two.

And word is on the street it is
and I have heard it said
that Bitm'kit and Whatshisface
are getting blooming wed.

Blimey girl I don't know that
I'm not a friend of theirs.
Who cares what the two of them
get up to up them stairs.

Hang on keep the noise down gal
I know that voice I do.
What Whatshisface can see in her
I haven't got a clue.

See gal, yeah you know her now
I knew you blooming would.
None forget old Bitm'kit
though many wish they could.

Aye that's her what flashed her drawers
at our new young M.P.
Poor boy still goes up to town,
he's getting therapy.

Well I'm off, it's Bingo gal
I'm due a winning line.
Got a feeling in me bones
that this will be my time.

Hang on, look at Bitm'kit,
it's got to be a joke.
That ain't Whatshisface she's with
she's got another bloke!

Where's me lippy, how's me hair
you got a mint on you?
I'll make a move on Whatshisface
before the Bingo's through.

A FLY IN MY SOUP

A fly in my soup,
it's looking quite pleased.
It's Alphabet soup
with carrots and peas.

The fly swims around
and then it goes under.
It's looking for something,
but what for, I wonder.

Flies don't eat carrots
and flies don't eat peas.
Flies live on rotting stuff,
flies spread disease.

Under it goes
it's right out of sight.
And then it is back...
Oh THAT can't be right.

It's dragged up some letters
of that there's no doubt.
It's spelled out a sentence;
'OH PLEASE GET ME OUT.'

SPIDERY THOUGHTS

Now spiders come to lessons
they're watching us it seems.
They're listening and learning
from up there in the beams.

Our teacher's like a spider
his limbs are spider thin.
His mouth is always open...
in case a fly pops in.

His desk has loads of cobwebs
he's got such staring eyes.
He's always eating currants...
which look like wingless flies.

He's very good at climbing
when we are in the gym.
It's really got me thinking...
I'll keep my eye on him.

SILVERADO

I flew off to America,
a dream inside my head
that I would find a pretty girl
and she and I would wed.

I landed at the airport
and then I saw her face.
I knew at once America
would be the perfect place.

I made my introduction
and we clicked straight away
we shared a coffee in the lounge
and chatted through the day.

She loved those Western movies
I said I like them too
the airport had a cinema
I knew just what to do.

The film was Silverado,
that film's one cut above.
It's length would give us loads of time
to madly fall in love.

Throughout the entire movie
she squeezed my hand so tight.
I gazed into her hazel eyes
oh, everything was right.

And when the movie finished
she said she was in love.
And I could hear those wedding bells
from somewhere up above.

Her eyes glowed with excitement,
as she stared into mine.
She said, "I'm off to Hollywood...
for I love Kevin Kline."

KETTLE LIDS

If little kids had kettle lids
and put them on their heads,
would it stop them dreaming
   as they lay in their beds?
Would it stop them laughing
   as they ran up the stair?
Stop them eating candy floss
   and getting sticky hair?
Stop them asking questions
like how and where and why?
Stop them wanting cuddles
   when they felt like a cry?
Stop them splashing water,
   but boil it up instead?
If little kids had kettle lids
and put them on their heads.

ENGLISH SPIDERS

English spiders might be hairy
English spiders may look scary
but there's something you should all be told.

English spiders have good breeding,
keep their mouths closed when they're feeding.
English spiders are as good as gold.

English spiders aren't appealing
in the bath tub, on the ceiling,
but they won't give anyone a bite.

They're not cuddly like a kitten,
but they have been born in Britain.
English spiders... cultured and polite.

AUNT MATILDA

Aunt Matilda's got a job
that suits her to the ground.
She loves telling people off
and bossing folks around.
Tourist Information
is just right for her I know.
Now she's getting paid
for telling people where to go!

JONATHON DORY

Oh this is the story
of Jonathon Dory,
a man who had only one wish.
To serve up a platter
of fish with no batter,
with peas on a herringbone dish.

The people around him
quite honestly found him
to be somewhat slow in the brain.
They'd all heard his chatter
of fish without batter,
again and again and again.

They laughed when they heard him,
but nothing deterred him.
He moved to a home on the coast.
Oh this is the story
of Jonathon Dory,
a man who was smarter than most.

He bought a blue trawler,
Old Rosie he called her
he sailed for a day and a night.
His hook it was baited,
he sat and he waited
for something to take a good bite.

He soon got his wish
for he landed a fish
that was larger than you'd ever think.
With hook in its throat
oh, it flapped on the boat,
and Old Rosie she started to sink.

Oh this is the story
of Jonathon Dory,
there's no-one as cunning as he.
He sat on the fish
that he craved for his dish,
and he rode it out into the sea.

He spotted some land
and he jerked with his hand,
oh the fish was too weak to resist.
He stepped from the sea
and he cried out with glee,
with the line firmly held in his fist.

But the smile on his face
it was quickly replaced
by a frown that was blacker than night.
For up there on the hill
stood an army quite still,
and they looked fairly fit for a fight.

And the captain rode down
and he said with a frown,
"You cannot come ashore with no pass."
So Jonathon said,
off the top of his head.
"I'm a chef of Imperial class."

Oh this is the story
of Jonathon Dory.
Whose wit was as sharp as a sword.
The captain alas
had the brain of an ass.
And he took the young man at his word.

Yes this is the story
of Jonathon Dory,
whose brain was as quick as a hawk.
He said "I must rest
for to cook at my best."
So he rode whilst the captain he walked.

They sent word ahead
to the king in his bed
that the chef soon to be at the gate...
would serve up a platter
of fish without batter,
with peas on a herringbone plate.

And the king was as fat
as a dairy maid's cat.
And his frown was as deep as a well.
His stomach was churning
and men of great learning
had tried every potion and spell.

"PLAIN FISH?" Roared the king.
"Never heard such a thing.
Call my doctor I need his advice."
So the doctor came in
and he said to the king,
that plain fish was in fact "very nice."

The doctor said fish
was a wonderful dish,
for it's full of all "Things that we need."
So the king gave a grin
that was WIDER than HIM.
"It's food fit for a king," he decreed.

Yes this is the story
of Jonathon Dory.
A man with one wish in his head.
And he soon got that wish
when he served up his dish
to the king as he sat in his bed.

The butler and maids
well they all looked afraid
as the king took his very first bite.
The soldiers stood near
with their swords and their spears,
and they had the new chef in their sights.

But the king did not speak
as he stuffed up his cheeks.
Oh he ate and he ate and he ate.
Then he burped out aloud
and he said to the crowd,
"Nothing's left, just this herringbone plate."

Oh the joy in the room
that was once full of gloom.
Oh the laughter just filled up that place.
The king crossed the mat
to where Jonathon sat
and quite loudly he burped in his face.

Then he said to the lad,
"That's the best meal I've had.
You're the best chef I've had here to date.
It was tender and white,
it was juicy and light.
I am sure I've already lost weight."

And a fan-fair was blown
as he sat on his throne,
and he offered the lad a great prize.
"My dear daughter," he said,
"is the one you shall wed,
she could do with a drop in dress size."

Oh the girl was as fat
as a cheese maker's cat,
but her smile was as sweet as could be.
And they wed right away
on that very same day,
on a boat floating out on the sea.

And he cooked for his wife
every day of his life.
And she cleared all the food from her plate.
Oh she loved every dish
be it chicken or fish.
And her dress size dropped down to an eight.

Oh that was the story
of Jonathon Dory.
A man who had only one wish.
To serve up a platter
of fish without batter,
with peas on a herringbone dish.

THE CURATE'S CAT

The Curate's cat
was very fat
the Curate never guessed...

He'd asked his wife
to feed the cat
the cat just did the rest...

The Curate's wife
had disappeared
the cat put on such weight...

The Curate's
searching for his wife...
the cat waits at the gate...

GOLDER'S GREEN

I caught a Hippopotamus
I should have caught a bus.
A Hippo doesn't stop at Golders Green.

It dropped me off at Kew
where stood a Kangaroo
a-chewing on a boomerang it seemed.

Easy thing to do,
jumpstart a Kangaroo
but this one took me back to where I'd been.

I took an Alligator
and thirty seconds later
I'm running for my life from teeth that gleam.

Another man might make it...
see a Hippo, take it
and get to where he really, really means.

I took a Hippopotamus
I should have caught a bus...
A Hippo NEVER stops at Golders Green.

JAPAN JAPAN

Japan, Japan you're years ahead,
the leaders in the race.
And even in America
they can't keep up the pace.

The go-word is technology
I bet you Japanese
were putting wheels on Subarus
while we still lived in trees.

Japan, Japan I'm gonna make
a visit to your shores.
I'll fill my brain with fresh ideas
to open up some doors.

You fly the flag of progress high
while we're still on our knees.
Oh what a gift you people have
to be born Japanese.

WANDA

I bought an anaconda
I went and called her Wanda
I used to keep tarantulas and bugs.
But spiders do not love ya
they think they are above ya
and no-one hugs me quite like Wanda hugs.

But then it turned out Wanda
was Wanda the absconder.
She cleared off and she took my hat and coat.
Now why would I be fibbin'?
She took off with my Gibbon
and neither one left me a goodbye note.

They made it to the station
and chose a destination.
They bought their tickets with my credit card.
Now I was never fonder
of anyone than Wanda
and living here without her will be hard.

Their journey soon was over
they'd caught the train to Dover.
They jumped upon the ferry to Calais.
Their ticket was a single
the Gibbon was bi-lingual.
He used his charm to help them on their way.

They met with no rejection
they'd planned it to perfection.
They caught a plane at airport Charles De Gaulle.
They set up home in Frisco
and opened up a bistro
where all the rich and famous came to call.

I was not too enamoured
my credit cards were hammered.
My banks were just as mad as they could get.
I almost stopped surviving
till cash began arriving.
The gibbon and the snake paid off my debt.

That money keeps arriving
I'm more than just surviving.
My seaside home is testament to that.
A parcel was delivered
it's contents made me shiver.
The snake returned my favourite coat and hat.

I bought an anaconda
I went and called her Wanda.
I used to keep tarantulas and bugs.
But spiders do not love ya
they think they are above ya.
Oh how I miss those anaconda hugs!

FAN MAIL

My fan sent me a flower
I put it in a cup.
I placed it on the mantelpiece
and topped the water up.

It bloomed all through the winter.
It bloomed all through the spring.
By summer folks were queuing up
to SEE the blooming thing.

My fan wrote me a letter
I only get the one.
So I thought I might write one back
to say what I had done.

I wrote the blooming letter.
I fed the blooming bloom.
I waited for an answer
oh I paced around my room.

The postman then delivered,
I fell down to the floor.
She said, "That plant is PLASTIC
please don't water anymore."

A DEVIL OF A DECISION

"I'm thinking of retiring," said the Devil.
"I've had enough of gluttony and greed.
There must be more to life than being evil,
a good long rest is just the thing I need."

"You can't just pack it in man!" God retorted.
"There has to be a Devil, don't you see?
For if there were no devious temptations,
then they would simply have no need for me!"

"You won't make me feel guilty," said the Devil.
"So far as guilt's concerned I am immune.
You tell me that you won't survive without me,
but when I'm gone you'll sing a different tune.

I cannot say I've not enjoyed our battle,
but I've decided now it's time to stop.
Besides, the odds were always stacked against you,
I'm getting out whilst I am still on top."

"I'll question that," the Lord replied with venom.
"Oh, lying sir it suits you very well.
On balance I have been much more successful,
I've saved more souls than you have dragged to Hell."

"Oh yes," the devil said; his eyes were gleaming.
"There are more souls in your place than in mine.
But that my dear is only human nature.
For most of them repented just in time.

"It's you who put that clause into the contract.
All men could be as sinful as could be.
But though you have them tucked up safe in Heaven,
their life on Earth was all mapped out by me!

And face it dear, they're not entirely happy.
Your knitting classes don't go down too well.
I know that if they had a second chance mate,
they'd vote for joining me down there in Hell.

For Hell is not all brimstone and hot fire,
unless of course, you count the barbecues.
No Hell is full of sin, and people love it.
Yes, Hell is full of gambling dens and booze.

My dear, if only you could see the faces
of all those reckless sinners who have died.
The ones who did not choose to be repentant,
their smiles could not be wider if they tried.

They're living in debauchery eternal.
Enjoying every moment now they're dead.
They pinch themselves each day, they can't believe it,
they think they've gone to Heaven dear instead.

But I have had enough and I am leaving.
A man can only party for so long."
He stood up to his feet and raised his trident.
Then with a flash of lightning, he was gone.

And down on Earth, there was no more temptation,
there was no jealousy or even greed.
And every single person loved their neighbour.
And no-one cared for more than they might need.

And peace swept through the lands as if a virus.
And not one person raised a hand for war.
The planet was engulfed with mutual caring,
and poverty and hunger were no more.

But mortal man is mortal for a reason,
and life will always lead to certain death.
And heaven was quite simply overcrowded,
as thousands every day took their last breath.

And what is more, they loved those knitting classes,
and righteous souls do not do things by halves.
They spent their days forever in hereafter,
by knitting miles and miles of Jesus scarves.

And God in all His wisdom was confounded,
as Heaven was so very nearly full.
But no-one now was going down to Hades,
and He was simply running out of wool.

And then from out of nowhere came the Devil.
"Retiring's not for me." he quickly said.
"Temptation now is back upon the menu,
those poor souls need some life after they're dead!"

And so the gates to Hell they were reopened.
And everything it seemed was as before.
Until they did a census up in Heaven,
and counted fewer souls instead of more.

So God himself stepped in to sort the problem.
But what He saw it made Him feel unwell.
The Jesus scarves were tied in knots together.
And souls were now escaping down to Hell!

BREAD AND JAM

Relax and I will tell a tale
you won't have heard before.
It's all about the NAFFI days
that I spent in the war.

The war was almost at an end
in northern Germany.
And we were down to bread and jam
for breakfast lunch and tea.

I toasted bread and warmed the jam
I served it cold and hot.
The men were far too hungry then,
to bother what they got.

And so the days grew into weeks
you do the best you can.
But bread will always be just bread
and jam is only jam.

And then one day a sergeant came
to mutter in my ear.
He had heard a whispered word
of food supplies quite near.

He did not know what food it was
it could be steak or ham.
But he was sure inside his bones
it was not currant jam.

The two of us took off that night
whilst all the soldiers slept.
We found the food inside a van
and in the back we crept.

We opened up the cases
and each one was filled with jars.
And every jar was labelled
Fine Beluga Caviar.

The truck had been abandoned
but its keys they were in place.
The sergeant and myself took turns
and drove it back to base.

Then all the jars were kitchen bound
we pledged our secrecy.
I'd give our men the finest meal
that there could ever be.

From colonel down to corporal
they sat at their breakfast seats.
And I served toast and caviar
a truly tasty treat.

They ate it down in silence
then they murmured just a bit.
They left the tent without a word
I nearly threw a fit.

I caught up with the colonel
and I strutted by his heel.
I asked him how his company
had taken to the meal.

"Oh it was fine," the colonel said,
"they really loved that dish.
But we all thought the currant jam
did taste a bit like fish!"

BAFFLED

Archangel Gabriel, him with the wings,
sits in the rafters and plaintively sings.
Black hearted monks chant a morbid repost
everyone's baffled but no-one is lost.
Ex TV comperes all sit at the bar,
drinking Martinis from recycled jars.
Then O J Simpson appears at the door,
making excuses for things gone before.
Gutter press newsmen sit by the spittoon,
fishing for scandal to fill their balloon.
Saddam Hussein does a turn on the stage...
rewriting history... burning the page.
Then Queen Elizabeth takes to the floor
showing off tattoos she won in the war.
Beefeaters hang from the overhead beams
handing out parcels of unwanted dreams.
Mickey Spillane with a cap in his hand
sings Leonard Cohen's So Long Marianne.
Hendrix and Lennon sit counting the cost,
everyone's baffled, but no-one is lost.

CHRISTMAS PRESENTS

Michael got a football,
Derek got a bat.
Steven got a rifle,
and a Winchester at that!
Eileen got some sewing stuff
to make a woollen mat.
Marion got a record,
and Marjie got a cat.
I got what I wanted...
A Davy Crockett hat!

Michael kicked his football,
just once and it went flat.
Steven broke his rifle,
and Derek lost his bat.
Marion's record jumped,
the cat ripped Eileen's mat.
Christmas day was bedlam,
sometimes it was like that.
I went off to bed...
in me Davy Crockett hat.

ZOMBIE REPELLENT

I'm making some Zombie repellent.
I've got the instructions right here.
I found this old book in the attic,
I've been out and fetched all the gear.

I found an old stove in the garden
I found a large pot in the shed.
And now I'm up here in the attic
I'm gonna repel the undead.

The slugs weren't too hard to get hold of,
the rat droppings they were a cinch.
It's piled up behind that old compost,
I didn't take more than an inch.

I couldn't find eyes of a toad though,
we don't have those toads around here.
But I found some smelly old mothballs,
those Zombies won't dare to come near.

I mixed all that stuff in my cauldron,
but cat wee was too hard to find.
Our cat's at the vets with a problem.
So I simply used some of mine.

I mixed in a measure of mustard
and dropped in some garlic as well.
And boy when I started to warm it
it gave off the stinkiest smell.

Some cheesy old socks of my brothers,
some farmyard manure from the shed.
Some eggs that were well past the use date
some cobwebs from under my bed.

The book said to stir for a fortnight,
I didn't have time for all that.
I borrowed Mum's new kitchen blender
and zapped it in three seconds flat.

I covered my nose with a hanky,
the pong filled my nose, filled my head.
Those Zombies won't know what has hit em...
one sniff and they'll wish they WERE dead.

This book that I found in the attic
I'm glad that I gave it a read.
It says that this Zombie repellent
is ninety per cent guaranteed.

I'm reading the final instructions
that's it I am packing it in.
The book says to tip out the potion
and rub it all over MY skin!

PANTOMIME

Life is but a pantomime
an act upon the stage.
Performed by one and everyone,
forever and an age.
And everybody gets a part;
to suit their style of course.
But since I joined I've always played
the back end of the Horse.

VAMPIRE PROOF PYJAMAS

I am not the type to make
a crisis from a drama
but why oh why does no-one make
some vampire proof pyjamas?

All it needs is just a touch
of garlic on the collar.
Patterns shaped like crosses,
oh, for just a few more dollars.

Everyone would sleep at night
relaxed and so much calmer.
Why oh why does no-one make
some vampire proof pyjamas?

GRANNY KNOT

My sister let her do it,
she has to take the blame.
Both of them just laughed at me
and said, "it's just a game."

I tried to stop her playing
and now it's gone to pot.
Her arms are where her legs should be.
Our granny's in a knot.

We both tried to untie her
but had to call a halt.
My sister let her do it though
it's all my sisters fault.

The ambulance came quickly,
the paramedics tried...
but after thirty minutes passed
the two of them just sighed.

"There's nothing we can do kids,"
the paramedics said,
"Her arms are where her legs should be
and we can't move her head."

"What you need is a sailor,"
they both went on to say.
"All sailors are real good at knots
they'll free her straight away."

Well, I looked down at granny.
Her skin had gone all white.
And every time she wriggled
all the knots became more tight.

So I ran to the dock yard.
and fetched back sailor Jim.
And when he saw my granny's plight
he gave the widest grin.

The sailor said "I'll do it,"
and started flexing thumbs.
"But I will want some payment though
and sailors work for rum."

The rum was in the sideboard
as plain as day to see.
But that gave us a problem
for our granny had the key.

"What we need is a Ferret."
Old Jim he said to me.
"We'll stuff it in that opening
between her thumb and knee."

And then our granny grunted,
"I cannot feel my thumbs.
My eyes are stuck wide open
and I'm staring at my bum."

So I ran to the pet shop,
and ferrets they had three.
But I came back with two
cos it was 'buy one get one free.'

We put them in position,
right close to granny's knee.
And one fetched out a ball of wool
the other had the key.

Then Jim drank down some liquor.
and then he drank the lot.
His fingers were a speeding blur
as he worked at the knots.

Just fourteen minutes later
our gran was all undone.
Old Jim the drunken sailor yelled,
"I've never had such fun."

So gran sat on the sofa,
and she looked pretty glum.
Too scared to open up her eyes
in case she saw her bum.

But Jim he seemed more sober.
He spoke to us quite plain,
"Well, one thing is for certain kids
you won't do that again.

By all means play with granny,'"
he whispered to my sister.
"Play Scrabble, even POKER girl
but don't let her play Twister!"

SHADOWS

Where do all the shadows go at night
as soon as you turn out the bedside light?
Do they hide in wardrobes
or crawl beneath the bed?
Do they creep beneath the sheets
and snuggle up instead?
They all just disappear at once
and far away from sight.
Oh where do all the shadows go at night?

Where do all the shadows go at night?
They simply disappear, it can't be right.
If I stretch out my arm
and turn my light back on,
the shadows simply stand around
as if they've not been gone.
I wouldn't want to race one
if they're all as fast as light.
Oh where do all the shadows go at night?

CUSTODY OF THE CAT

I have our cat, called Claws,
I wish that he were yours.

He's sitting on my knee,
I just can't prise him free.

When you were here, my dear,
this cat would not come near.

But then you flew the nest
and left me with this pest.

There's water in my eyes,
the blood runs down my thighs.

I have our cat, called Claws,
I wish that he were yours!

SPRING IN MY STEP

I walked from the house
with a spring in my step
and a light hearted song on my lips.
And I would have skipped
all the way into town
if it just hadn't been for my hips.

If it just hadn't been
for the pain in my back
oh I just couldn't move through the gears.
My mind it was willing
to give it a go...
but my body had other ideas.

So I walked into town
and I held my head high
and I took in the warmth of the breeze.
Oh I would have danced
to the song of the thrush...
if it just hadn't been for my knees.

Well, I got into town
though it took me some time
and I sat on a bench for a while.
And I would have stayed there
for quite a long time...
if it just hadn't been for my piles.

And I watched the young boys
skimming stones on the pond
and I smiled as they laughed on that day.
Then I closed up my eyes
for a much clearer view
and I joined in their innocent play.

With a spring in my step
and a head full of dreams
and no burden of life that's passed by.
I was twelve once again
for a moment or two...
I could dance, I could skip, I could FLY.

Then I turned to the path
with a spring in my step
that was hard to define or to gauge.
And I would have run
every yard up that hill,
if it just had not been for my age.

THE DOGS AND CATS

The dogs and cats could not agree
they held a meeting by the sea.
With narrow eyes and wrinkled frown
they weighed each other up and down.

Each dogged dog and crafty cat
upon a velvet cushion sat.
They did not scratch they did not bite.
They knew they had to do this right.

They brought some bags they brought one each.
The sea lapped up onto the beach.
They put up parasols for shade
and shared out cans of lemonade.

They had to even out the scores
they sucked the soda through the straws.
They had some doughnuts freshly baked
some biscuits and some chocolate cake.

And as the first one made his speech
a bowl was handed out to each.
They shared a trifle equally
and held their meeting by the sea.

Their meeting lasted through the night
the moon shone down with silver light.
The dogs and cats had made a vow
to solve their problems here and NOW!

They lit a fire to warm their feet
and toast marshmallows soft and sweet.
They did not spit they did not bark
the fire spat; the fire sparked.

They did not howl they did not screech,
they fell asleep upon the beach.
The dogs and cats could not agree,
they held a meeting by the sea.

They did not sort it out that's plain...
but DID agree to meet again.

A BRILLIANT IDEA

Disaster round at granny's house,
just me and her for tea.
She's gone and lost her hearing aid
wherever could it be?

We searched the house all over
from the bottom to the top.
Without it she would never hear
a BOMB if it should drop.

But then I had what dad would call
a brilliant idea.
So good that it would matter not
if granny couldn't hear.

I knew that she would ask me
what I wanted for my tea.
I wrote my answer down in letters
big as big could be.

And so when granny asked me
what I wanted to be fed.
I held up my paper sheet...
She stared at it and said.

"A brilliant idea my boy
but you'll still have to yell,
'cause when I lost me hearing aid...
I lost me specs as well."

Printed in Great Britain
by Amazon

83064449R00041